Social Skills

for primary pupils ①

Seven one-hour sessions to help pupils develop social awareness and personal responsibility

Deborah Cohen and Lorrae Jaderberg

Social Skills for Primary Pupils 1
MT10774
ISBN-13: 978 1 85503 448 8

© Deborah Cohen and Lorrae Jaderberg
Illustrations © Dusan Pavlic
Music recorded by Zig Zag Productions
Singers: George Lawton, Angus Rea, Eloise Rea and Holly Turner
All rights reserved
First published 2008
Reprinted 2014, 2015, 2017, 2018

Printed by Page Bros, Norwich, UK
Pintail Close, Victoria Business Park, Nottingham, NG4 2SG

Contents

About the authors

Deborah Cohen

Deborah Cohen is an advisory teacher for pupils with autism. She has a post-graduate diploma in specific learning difficulties and was a SENCo in two primary schools. Deborah has also worked for Parent Partnership, advising parents of children with special educational needs, and was a primary teacher in Barnet, north London, for 20 years.

Lorrae Jaderberg

Lorrae Jaderberg is an educational consultant. She has previously held posts as a deputy head teacher and inclusion manager at a north London primary school, a SENCo and a class teacher.

Acknowledgements

Colin McGee
DipPsych, UKCP Reg, DHpPsych (UK), GQHP, Reg Hyp (GHR) CertEd

Woodridge Primary School, London
Moira Shaw (head teacher), Sue Newland, pupils and staff

St Mary's & St John's CE Primary School, London
Dee Oelman (head teacher), Yvonne Richards, Charlotte Over, pupils and staff

The Hyde Primary School, London
Jo Hester (head teacher), Di Jolley, Claudette Brown, pupils and staff

Brunswick Park Primary School, London
Marian Hossell (head teacher), Giovanna Phelan, Dianne Stanley, Cath Coombs, pupils and staff

Adult's guide

What is Social Skills for Primary Pupils 1?

Social Skills for Primary Pupils is a programme to help children develop social awareness and understanding of their interactions and responsibility for their own and others' behaviour. It supports and enhances the government's Every Child Matters initiative, which focuses on how to be healthy, safe, enjoy and achieve, make a positive contribution, and achieve economic well-being.

Social Skills for Primary Pupils 1 explores the story of a group of children who want to make their school a better place. Each time, over seven sessions, pupils learn a new skill which they practise through games, role-play and discussion. In each session pupils colour in a skills token which they use to make their own poster in Session 7 to remind them of the skills learned, and take the relevant classroom poster slip back to the classroom to display. During each session they also learn a verse and actions to the song 'We know how to ...'.

The homework activities and classroom poster are designed to promote the programme's skills across school and home settings.

Over the seven sessions, pupils build up personal experience through discussion, games and exercises informed by adult and peer feedback. Sessions cover National Curriculum PSHE and Citizenship guidelines. The Primary National Strategy (*Excellence and Enjoyment: Learning and Teaching in the Primary Years*) and Social and Emotional Aspects of Learning (SEAL) affirm a vision for primary education that recognises the importance of social skills in creating effective conditions for learning. The following social skills are included:

- recognising what they like and dislike, what is fair and unfair, and what is right and wrong (Sessions 2 and 6);

- sharing opinions on things that matter to them (all sessions), explaining their views (all sessions);

- recognising, naming and dealing with their feelings in a positive way (Session 4);

- recognising choices they can make, and the difference between right and wrong (Session 2);

- recognising that they belong to various groups and communities, such as family and school (Session 1);

- recognising how their behaviour affects others (Session 3);

- listening to others, and playing and working cooperatively (Sessions 1 and 6);

- identifying and respecting the differences and similarities between people (Session 5).

66 My school wants to adopt 'We know how to ...' as our school song. 99

66 All the children in the class have been saying 'Good choice, bad choice.' 99

66 The programme fits in so well with SEAL. 99

66 It develops the emotional literacy that SEAL promotes, giving the children the vocabulary to express how they feel. 99

Why was this programme developed?

Social Skills for Primary Pupils was developed as part of inclusive primary practice. There is a growing need for social skills intervention in the primary years. During the sessions the pupils learn about their strengths and weaknesses and how these may help them grow and develop. Pupils learn from their peers and adult supporter by a process of gradually heightened self-awareness. They learn how to deal with their specific weaknesses and with issues relating to conflict resolution, friendships and behaviour in the playground and in class.

This programme may lead on to further specialised group or one-to-one work, either in school or provided by outside agencies.

> 66 The children are getting much better at describing how they feel. One child said to a classmate, 'Stop saying that about me. It makes me feel upset.' 99

What is behind it?

Pupils' self-esteem and social and emotional well-being is central to their ability to fulfil their academic, social and emotional potential. The Primary National Strategy and SEAL suggest that many primary pupils struggle with social and emotional issues which significantly affect their confidence and ability to perform at school. Using our own experience and informed by current research, we have designed this programme to support the learning of complex social interactions in school.

> 66 The programme linked very well with the SEAL materials. 99

How does it work?

We know that children are motivated and learn best when they feel safe and in control of their learning. This programme is designed to enable pupils to develop an understanding of the themes of the sessions and learn strategies to deal with issues at their own level of awareness, involvement and pace. Elements of the programme may be adapted to suit individuals. It may be used in small groups and whole classes.

Why does it work?

This programme builds on individual and group trust, confidentiality and peer/adult support. It allows pupils to explore relevant challenging social and emotional issues in safety.

> 66 The programme was very valuable. We saw a child who had no friends, made no eye contact and was an outsider make huge strides in a short space of time. 99

The sessions are structured and paced in such a way that pupils will operate from their own level of personal development. By the second one pupils relax as they recognise the framework of the previous session. They begin to build up trust, which enables them to utilise the framework to support experimentation with their new social skills in a safe environment. The framework also provides ongoing opportunities for self-evaluation, challenge and target setting to take place.

> 66 We have noticed how the children share now. 99

Praise and encouragement are central to the sessions. As a result, pupils' self-esteem and motivation increase as they build on their successes and look forward to the next session and the challenges it will bring. By the end of the seven sessions, pupils report that they feel more confident in dealing with specific issues and have a clearer understanding of how their own strengths and weaknesses affect them. They develop additional strategies to support themselves.

What does the programme consist of?

The *Social Skills for Primary Pupils 1* programme consists of seven 50-minute to 1-hour interactive sessions. These may be held over days, weeks or months. Each session has a resource list, adult's script and evaluation grids. There are also classroom poster and poster slips, pupil posters, tokens, photocopiable resources and a song on CD. An adult skills-rating form is completed before the programme starts and reviewed at the end of Session 7. There is also a pupil self-rating questionnaire to be completed before and after the programme so that pupils can evaluate how it has helped them.

Each session focuses on specific issues presented in short activities – games, discussions, problem-solving, collaborative reflection, working in pairs and creating conclusions. The activities are designed to help pupils relax, bond as a group and stimulate discussion. There is a homework reinforcement activity that pupils report back on at the next session.

> **The whole class wanted to come each week.**

Each session includes a story that says what the children did next to make their school a better place. This introduces the session's focus. After the games and activities, pupils colour in the relevant token. They learn the next verse and actions of 'We know how to ...' using the CD.

> **The class teacher used the class poster with the whole class, and they learned the song and actions as part of PSHE.**

At the end of each session the adult writes a comment and scores each pupil's contribution on the Adult evaluation grid. These evaluations are a valuable record that may help the class teacher, outside agencies, educational psychologist and parents/carers. They may be used for planning and developing future social skills work.

During Session 7 each pupil creates a poster from the tokens they have coloured in. The poster shows the focus of each session and provides a reminder of all that has been achieved. The pupils are usually very proud of their poster, and may like to decorate it with glitter and stickers. With their agreement, their work may be displayed. Some pupils may decline as this may be sensitive and private work. Adults should emphasise that to decline is acceptable. The classroom poster will also have been completed and will be on display.

> **Taking the poster back to class each week was important and gave the programme credibility.**

A certificate of achievement is presented to participants as an acknowledgement of their efforts. A small gift may also be presented.

The Pupil self-rating questionnaire should be filled in before the programme starts. The adult may sit with each pupil to help them to complete it. Pupils will revisit their questionnaire in Session 7, repeating the scaling exercise so that they can evaluate the progress they feel they have made. This generates discussion, and the information may be used to inform future planning.

Who should run the group?

As this is a complex area of primary children's development, it is recommended that someone with experience in dealing with conflict resolution, mediation and self-esteem issues runs the group. This may be a member of staff whose personal or professional strengths lie in this area, such as a trained counsellor, teaching assistant, support teacher, SENCo, deputy head or head teacher.

Sessions are designed to be led and evaluated by one person. Schools may choose to run sessions with two adults, one leading the session and the other observing and taking notes for evaluation purposes. This offers an opportunity to train new adults to run groups. Some schools have found it beneficial to run all of the groups with two adults so that, in the event of a pupil raising painful or distressing issues during a session, one adult can support the individual pupil whilst the other adult continues with the group.

The benefits of the programme are greatest when it forms part of a whole-school approach. Ideally all staff should be included in an initial training session which explains the aims and methodology so that they can help pupils to transfer skills learned within the group into different settings in school. At the very least, all teachers and teaching assistants working directly with pupils in the group should be briefed about the programme and be made aware of pupils' targets so that they can support and encourage those pupils in acting appropriately in school.

> **All the children who participated are very proud of themselves, and the others are asking when they can have a turn.**

When and where should the sessions take place?

Group sessions should take place at a time which the class teacher judges appropriate. Whole-class sessions should be planned as part of the PSHE curriculum. Group sessions should take place in a private and quiet environment.

Who should be in the group?

A group should ideally consist of six to eight children, comprising two or three model pupils, the same number of quiet pupils, and two target pupils whose needs are complementary (or one target pupil).

> **It was an opportunity for pupils to share ideas about what to do and say in situations they had encountered.**

When a pupil is having social or emotional difficulties in school that are a serious cause of concern for the parent, teaching assistant, class teacher, SENCo or the pupil themselves, these pupils may benefit from being part of a group. Sometimes pupils' self-esteem may be affected by problems outside school rather than by a specific school-based issue. Pupils in this category will also benefit from this form of social skills intervention.

Guidelines for choosing members of the group are outlined on page 9. It is important that groups are balanced so that each participant gains the maximum benefit from the programme.

Elements of self-esteem

During the seven sessions the programme addresses various elements of self-esteem, such as:

> **Gary has started to work with other children for the first time.**

- unconditional self-acceptance
- sense of capability and purpose
- appropriate assertiveness
- experience of flow and fulfilment
- sense of responsibility and accountability
- sense of safety and security
- sense of belonging
- sense of integrity.

Challenge, inclusion, learning styles and self-evaluation

Central to *Social Skills for Primary Pupils 1* is inclusive practice. Pupils are able to access the materials and are challenged at the level appropriate for them. This is a multi-sensory programme and we have found it suits all learning styles. Pupils with English as an additional language are encouraged to ask for help if necessary in understanding the tasks and should be prepared ahead of time with vocabulary rehearsal. The focus skills may be written in a pupil's home language. The adult running the group may adapt the language used in the script according to the needs of the group with which they are working.

Pupils are encouraged to move at their own pace, challenging themselves at their own level. *Social Skills for Primary Pupils 1* is suitable for pupils aged 6–8 years, but has been used with older pupils too.

Developing self-evaluation skills is a key part of the programme. Pupils are encouraged to consider perceptions of themselves and their behaviour alongside peers' views in order to develop and build an accurate picture of themselves, their social skills and their strengths and weaknesses. This is about building and strengthening the 'observing self' within each child, promoting empathy and a sense of community.

At the end of the programme, some children may mark themselves down in some areas when repeating the Pupil self-rating questionnaire. This is often because they marked themselves too high at the start of the programme as they didn't have an accurate understanding of their own abilities. This outcome is a useful discussion point.

Starting a group

Use the Checklist for running the group (**PCM 1**) to help you.

Explain the purpose of the sessions to the class teacher and ask for their help to select the group (**PCM 2**).

Find a suitable day and time for the group to meet.

The general purpose of the sessions will be to support and develop the social skills of one or two pupils who have been identified as specifically needing this sort of intervention. Two pupils should have complementary needs. Quiet, reserved pupils are included to develop their assertiveness skills. Model pupils are chosen in order to demonstrate the appropriate responses to the exercises in each session and to reduce the possibility of the children being identified as a 'naughty group'. The group might therefore comprise:

- primary target pupil and secondary target pupil
- two 'quiet' pupils • two model pupils.

The group should consist of a similar number of boys and girls.

It is important to maintain the balance of the group as outlined above. Groups should contain a maximum of two 'target' pupils in order to be effective.

> **❝It was good to have a script that allowed opportunities for me to add my own words. ❞**

> **❝By Session 6 she had improved her listening skills, was relaxed and engaged, and was able to say 'I don't know' when asked a question – something she would not have done before. ❞**

> **❝The evaluation grids were really valuable in keeping track of changes in behaviour.❞**

> **❝The class teacher was actively involved and was great at praising the children in class.❞**

Letter to parents/carers (**PCM 3**) Once the pupils have been chosen, send a letter home explaining the programme and homework. Give them the choice of opting out of the programme.

Invitation to pupil (**PCM 4**) After a short time to allow parents/carers to opt out, send a personal invitation to each pupil.

Adult skills-rating form (**PCM 5**) Together with the class teacher, complete a form for each pupil. The class teacher rates each at the end of the programme, using the same form to compare scores.

Pupil self-rating questionnaire (**PCM 6**) In a 20-min. preliminary session, explain how the group will run. They may choose a name. Get the pupils to complete the Pupil self-rating questionnaire. In Session 7 they rate themselves again on it. Ask them to place stickers on the lines to represent the level of skill they feel they have against the statements. To make sure they understand the task, ask them to point first to where they want to place their sticker. They rate themselves again on their sheet in Session 7.

Record-keeping

Take the register at the beginning of each session. Pupils may be asked to share examples of what they have practised since the previous session. After each session, complete an adult evaluation grid (**PCM 7**) for each pupil. The grid records, on a scale of 1–5 (1 is lowest) the role and participation of each pupil in the session; roles may be defined as one of the following, and may change in and between sessions. The evaluation grids provide an overview of roles, participation and behaviour. The information may be used as evidence of development.

66 The programme's structure and organisation was simple to follow and I adapted it to suit my group with ease when necessary. 99

Leader – consistently takes the lead through discussions, initiates questions, offers solutions and supports others.

Group member – shows sensitivity to other members and staff, follows the rules and makes valuable contributions.

Follower – finds difficulty expressing opinions or joining in activities without others having shown an example or offered their opinion first.

Participant – joins in everything, includes others, complies with rules, often makes suggestions and takes initiative.

Disrupter – strays from the focus, involves themselves in activities that distract from the focus activity, causes disruption.

Aggressor – brings about aggressive interventions, stopping the group from functioning peacefully and affecting others' behaviour.

Scapegoat – allows themselves to become victim of other pupils' difficulties, unable to withstand or respond with resilience.

Evaluate your own input after each session and make notes for next time. Praise pupils to encourage self-confidence and self-esteem. You may give out reward stickers to encourage participation and acknowledge positive contributions.

Follow-up

For some pupils, the social skills group is the first opportunity they will have to examine their own feelings and have others value their experiences and ideas. Many schools will be keen to build on this positive experience and to give pupils further opportunities to develop their personal growth.

When the programme has been completed, on the basis of their evaluations schools may decide that further intervention is required for specific pupils. Some of the follow-up work undertaken by schools using this programme is described below:

- A pupil was referred on to other agencies for in-depth therapeutic input.

- A pupil was given additional one-to-one time to practise strategies to use in the classroom and playground.

- A parent support group was set up to run parallel to the social skills group. Parents were able to find out more about the skills that their children were learning and ways to support the work of the school by ensuring a consistent approach at home.

- A school followed up the programme by offering a 'talk time' in which pupils could book a 15-minute slot with the group leader to talk about any issues that were of concern to them or just to spend time reinforcing the work that had been done in the group.

- The group met up again every half-term to talk about their experiences.

- Schools may choose to use the *Social Skills for Primary Pupils 2* programme in the following year to develop pupils' skills further.

At the end of the programme, you may decide to hold a ceremony to mark the occasion. Some schools hold a class or whole-school assembly during which pupils participating in the programme show their posters, talk about the work they have done and teach the other pupils the group song, including actions.

Adapting the programme

"The material is adaptable and very easy to follow."

The order and content of the sessions are flexible and may be tailored to the needs of individuals and the group. You may wish to devise additional sessions following the same format.

After becoming familiar with the programme, some schools adapted the content to reflect issues specific to their circumstances. One group discussed how emotions make you feel inside. They made a life-size poster of a person with textured materials to represent the different emotions they might feel – rough pan-scourers to represent anger, soft sponge for contentment.

"The programme is very flexible. I was able to spend longer on some aspects if I needed to."

We welcome feedback and are always delighted to hear how schools have extended or adapted the programme. Please send such information and any accompanying photographs to hatley20@yahoo.co.uk

PCM 1:
Checklist for running the group

Action	Date of action	Notes
Prepare materials for programme.		
Choose pupils in collaboration with class teachers (**PCM 2**).		
Send out letters to parents/carers (**PCM 3**).		
Review parent/carer responses.		
Send invitations to pupils (**PCM 4**).		
Teachers/adults fill out Adult skills-rating forms (**PCM 5**).		
Initial meeting with pupils to introduce programme.		
Pupils fill out Pupil self-rating questionnaires (**PCM 6**).		
Session 1		
Session 2		
Session 3		
Session 4		
Session 5		
Session 6		
Session 7 – pupils review Pupil self-rating questionnaires.		
Class/school assembly to show posters and teach song.		
Adult fills out Adult skills-rating forms.		
Review all evaluations and plan any follow-up.		

SOCIAL SKILLS GROUP

To: Class: Date:

From:

Re: Social Skills Group

The target pupil for this group is ....

Please would you choose other children to join the group.

The group will start on ....

The group will meet for seven one-hour sessions.

Two model pupils ....

Two quiet pupils ....

One other pupil who would benefit from a social skills group

....

Please advise your preferred time for the group to meet:

Day of week .... Lesson ....

Please return this form by ....

Thank you.

Date:

DEAR PARENT/CARER

As part of the Key Stage 1 Personal, Social and Health Education (PSHE) and Citizenship curriculum, children learn about themselves as developing individuals and as members of their community. Your child has been chosen to participate in a group starting on ....

The group consists of about six children who will work together with me for seven one-hour sessions, concentrating on specific social skills relating to good listening, making choices, thinking about themselves and others, expressing their feelings, respecting differences and working together.

The children in the group have been chosen to complement each other. They practise desired behaviour, contribute to thought-provoking discussion and are encouraged to give appropriate feedback.

Each week your child will be practising a different skill. We will send home a note telling you what we have been working on. I should be grateful if you would praise and encourage your child when you notice them using these skills.

This is a special opportunity for your child. If you do not wish your child to participate in this group, please let me know as soon as possible so that another pupil may be offered the place. The children will attend sessions on

....

....

If you would like further information, please contact me.

I am looking forward to working with your child.

Yours sincerely

PCM 4:
Invitation to pupil

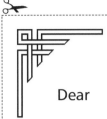
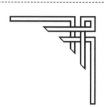

Dear

Class ...

You are invited to join our special group for social skills.

This group will help to make our school a better place.

We shall play games and have fun talking. You will also make a poster to keep.

I am looking forward to working with you.

Yours

Dear

Class ...

You are invited to join our special group for social skills.

This group will help to make our school a better place.

We shall play games and have fun talking. You will also make a poster to keep.

I am looking forward to working with you.

Yours

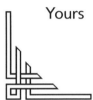

PCM 5:
Adult skills-rating form

Name of child: ....

Circle the statements that are true in relation to:
a) adults b) other children

Start date: ....

End date: ....

They are able to:

		🙁		😐		🙂
1 listen actively to others	adults	1	2	3	4	5
	children	1	2	3	4	5
2 repair damaged relationships	adults	1	2	3	4	5
	children	1	2	3	4	5
3 express their feelings	adults	1	2	3	4	5
	children	1	2	3	4	5
4 help others	adults	1	2	3	4	5
	children	1	2	3	4	5
5 understand how others feel	adults	1	2	3	4	5
	children	1	2	3	4	5
6 be an active member of the class		1	2	3	4	5
7 understand the difference between right and wrong		1	2	3	4	5
8 play fairly with other children		1	2	3	4	5

PCM 6:
Pupil self-rating questionnaire

Name: ....

Put a sticker on each line to show how you feel.

Start date: ....

End date: ....

Statement	😊	😐	🙁
I am able to express my feelings			
I feel confident			
I am able to listen			
I am able to understand other people's feelings			
I am able to deal with difficult situations			
I feel part of the group/class			
Other people understand me			
I have fun and play with others			

PCM 7:
Adult evaluation grid

Pupil's name: ....

Describe role within group: leader (L), group member (GM), follower (F), disrupter (D), participant (P), aggressor (A), scapegoat (S).

See page 10 for further guidance.

Score columns on a 1–5 scale (1 low and 5 high).

Session number	Attendance and homework	Describe role within group	Relationship with peers 1–5 scale	Response to adults 1–5 scale	Joining in activities 1–5 scale	Comments
1						
2						
3						
4						
5						
6						
7						

Something I learned ....

Something I do differently now ....

Something I found difficult ....

Something I enjoyed ....

Session 1 Listening

Resources

- pencils ● crayons ● a mirror per child
- Good listening tokens (**PCM 8**) – one token per child
- 'We know how to ...' lyrics (**PCM 9**), CD2 and a CD player
- Homework for Session 1 (**PCM 10**) – one slip per child
- We listen well classroom poster slip(s) (**PCM 11**) – Blu-Tack® on back
- Classroom poster – one per class represented (**PCM 12**)
- Adult evaluation grid – one per child

Aims

- To enable the group to begin to form and develop a common understanding and purpose
- To recognise that they belong to various groups and communities
- To begin taking responsibility for their actions
- To think about why it is important to listen, and to recognise what good listening means
- To take part in a discussion and share their opinions

Introduction 1 min.

Take the register and say hello to everyone in the group.

Belonging 5 mins.

This establishes the group and gives pupils a sense of belonging.

How lovely to see you all sitting so beautifully waiting to start. What a lovely group of children we have today. We're going to start by talking about all the groups we belong to. We don't just belong to this group. All of us belong to lots of different groups in and out of school. This group is also part of year(s) .... of .... school. What other groups do you belong to?

Prompt pupils to suggest other groups they belong to, such as their family, friendship groups, religious groups, organisations with people with similar attributes, and so on.

Isn't it lovely to know that we are part of so many different groups? We also do things together, such as looking after each other and sharing the same interests.

Today I'm going to tell you about a group of children who decided that they wanted to make their school a better place. They started to think of things they might do. What do you think they might do?

> **"I liked listening to other people speaking."**

Introducing the story: Making our school a better place 5 mins.

This activity encourages pupils to share ideas and consider the views of others. Encourage the pupils to share their ideas. Acknowledge suggestions such as having toys in the playground by saying:

That's an interesting idea.

I like that idea – remember that for later.

Explore general suggestions relating to pupil behaviour and encourage specific responses:

That's a good idea. What kind of things would they do to behave better?

Continue the story.

One of the ways the children decided to make their school a better place was to practise listening carefully.

Why is listening important?

When do you need to listen to other people?

Whom should you listen to?

Why did you suggest those people?

Acknowledge and discuss any suggestions.

The children in the story wanted to learn how to listen well, so they decided to practise. They found someone in the group to work with. They took it in turn to speak while their partner looked at them and paid attention.

Good listening 5 mins.

This activity encourages pupils to be aware of what listening is.

I want you to watch me speaking to .... Pay attention to what I do when I'm speaking and what they do while they're listening.

Model speaking to a pupil.

Hello, ... I hope you had a nice weekend. I did. I took ...., my dog, to the park.

What did I look like when I was speaking? What kind of things did I do?

What was .... doing when I was speaking?

Tease out the features of good listening – looking at the person, making eye contact, thinking about what they are saying, nodding, smiling.

Show me what a listening face looks like, ... That's very good, I can see you looking and watching carefully.

Looking in a mirror `5 mins.`

This activity encourages pupils to recognise body language and facial expressions that indicate to others that they are listening.

I'm going to give each of you a mirror so you can look at yourself making a listening face.

Hand out a mirror to each pupil.

Have a good look at your reflection so that you will remember what you look like when you're listening. How do I know you are listening? What are you doing that shows me you are listening?

I can see you are concentrating. What else are you doing? Will you remember how to make the same face later?

Collect in the mirrors.

❝I was wriggling on the carpet, but then I stopped and listened.❞

Practising good listening `10 mins.`

It's your turn to practise good listening now.

Ask pupils to stand in a circle and sort them into pairs. Call one child in each pair Child A and the other Child B.

All As, put your hand up. All Bs, put your hand up. Excellent, you listened carefully. Put your hands down. Turn to face your partner. A is going to tell their partner what their favourite meal is. See if you can describe it really well so that your partner feels hungry! I want to see all the partners listening carefully.

After a minute stop the pupils and discuss what constitutes good listening. Ask the pupils what didn't work and what they could do instead. Swap roles in the pairs and repeat the activity.

Listening game `5 mins.`

This activity consolidates the skills needed to listen effectively.

Go round the circle and ask each pupil in turn to say what their favourite food is. Next, point to a pupil and call out their name. The rest of the group then shout out that pupil's favourite food.

Well done, now who'd like to do the choosing?

Pick a pupil to take your role and repeat the game.

Well done. How did we remember everyone's favourite food?

That's right, because we were listening. When you go back to your class(es), how will your teacher know you are listening?

Yes, that's right. You'll be looking, listening, nodding, sitting still, concentrating.

Colour in today's token and listen to CD 5 mins.

This kinaesthetic activity reinforces the skills learned in the session.

Show the pupils the Good listening token. Each pupil colours in their token while listening to the backing track on the audio CD. Ask them to write their name on the back of their token. Explain that you will keep the tokens for now, and pupils will use them soon to help to make their school a better place.

Summary 1 min.

We're already starting to make our school a better place. We're going to think of a different way to make our school a better place each week for the next six sessions, as the children in the story did.

Each time, one of you may take a piece of the poster we'll be creating back to your classroom as a reminder of what we are doing to make the school a better place. Each of you will take a note for your parents or carers home so that they know what you are doing to make our school a better place.

What do you think they will think about your excellent listening skills? How will they notice?

Next time, I'm going to ask you how you got on with your listening. Don't forget to practise so you can tell us about how you got on. If you want to, you can draw a picture to show us next time. It might help you to remember when you practised good listening.

We're going to practise listening to our teacher and to each other this time. We've got a song that will help us remember what to do.

66 Now I think about things in class. 99

'We know how to ...' 5 mins.

Listen to the first verse of the song on the audio CD. Teach the pupils the words and actions. Repeat together until the children can confidently join in.

Homework 2 mins.

Give out homework. Nominate one pupil per class to take the We listen well slip to their classroom, along with the Classroom poster.

Final listening activity 1 min.

Line up at the door if you have ... blue eyes, white socks, glasses.

Evaluate the session using the Adult evaluation grid for each pupil.

PCM 8: Good listening tokens

Good listening

Good listening

Good listening

Good listening

Good listening

Good listening

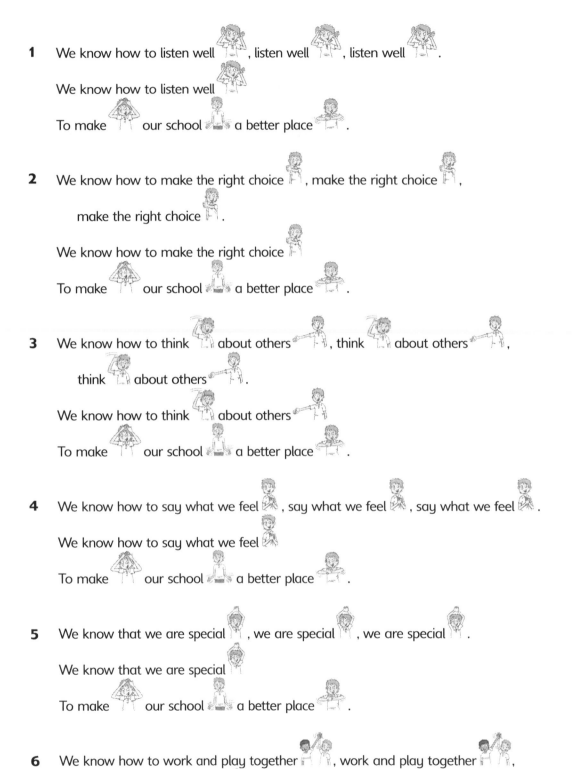

1 We know how to listen well , listen well , listen well .

We know how to listen well

To make our school a better place .

2 We know how to make the right choice , make the right choice ,

make the right choice .

We know how to make the right choice

To make our school a better place .

3 We know how to think about others , think about others ,

think about others .

We know how to think about others

To make our school a better place .

4 We know how to say what we feel , say what we feel , say what we feel .

We know how to say what we feel

To make our school a better place .

5 We know that we are special , we are special , we are special .

We know that we are special

To make our school a better place .

6 We know how to work and play together , work and play together ,

work and play together .

We know how to work and play together

To make our school a better place .

This week we have been working on **listening**.

Please praise and encourage your child when they use their listening skills.

Your child may choose to draw a picture of themselves to show one of the times they listened carefully since Session 1.

This week we have been working on **listening**.

Please praise and encourage your child when they use their listening skills.

Your child may choose to draw a picture of themselves to show one of the times they listened carefully since Session 1.

This week we have been working on **listening**.

Please praise and encourage your child when they use their listening skills.

Your child may choose to draw a picture of themselves to show one of the times they listened carefully since Session 1.

PCM 11: Classroom poster slips

We listen well.

We make the right choices.

We think about others.

We know how we feel.

We are special.

We work and play together.

PCM 12: Classroom poster

Photocopy both pages on A3 card to make the background for the poster.

We are making our school a better place.

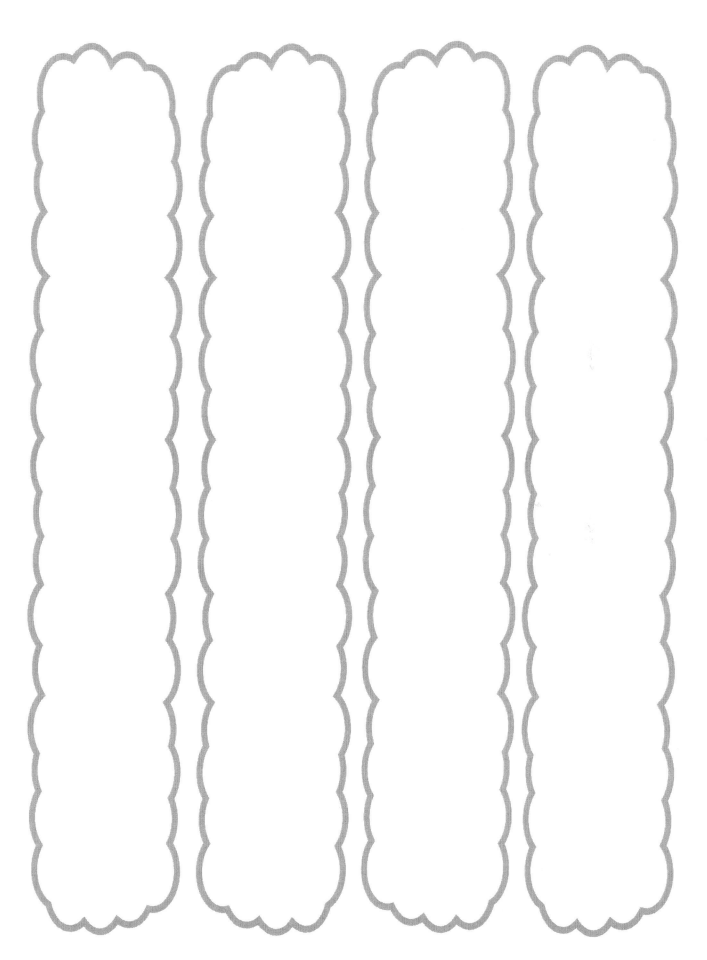

Session 2:
Making the right choice

Resources

- pencils • crayons
- Choice picture cards (**PCM 13**)
- Right choice tokens (**PCM 14**)
- 'We know how to ...' lyrics, CD2 and a CD player
- Homework for Session 2 (**PCM 15**)
- We make the right choices classroom poster slip(s) (**PCM 11**)
- Adult evaluation grids

Aims

- To recap on last session's theme
- To know they have choices
- To practise making choices
- To recognise the difference between right and wrong
- To begin to recognise the feelings we have when choosing our actions
- To take part in a discussion and share their opinions

Introduction 1 min.

Take the register and say hello to everyone in the group.

Review homework 5 mins.

Who would like to tell us about when they listened well this week?

Encourage pupils to share their stories and show any pictures they have drawn. Use descriptive praise to reinforce the appropriate behaviours, such as the following:

I imagine your teacher noticed how you looked at them and thought that you were concentrating on what they were saying. They must have been very pleased.

I'm sure your mum/classmate/carer was pleased that you listened so carefully and remembered what they said. I think the school is a much better place with you listening so well. I hope the other children will follow your lead. You will have to show them how to listen as you do.

The story continued `1 min.`

You may wish to show one of the Good listening tokens coloured in during Session 1 as a visual prompt.

Once there was a group of children who wanted to make their school a better place. Do you remember what the first thing that they decided to do was? Yes, well done, good listening [perform the listening action from 'We know how to ...' – cup your hands round your ears]. *Who would like to show us what good listening looks like?*

So, first they practised good listening. [Repeat action].

Next, the children decided to practise making good choices.

So, they played a little game, which we're going to play too.

Game: Thumbs up, thumbs down `10 mins.`

This game helps to explore whether actions are right or wrong.

Demonstrate the thumbs-up and thumbs-down signs. Explain that thumbs up indicates a good choice and thumbs down a poor choice.

The teacher is talking to the class and the children are looking at them and listening carefully. Have the children made a good choice or a poor choice?

Is that thumbs up or thumbs down?

Take answers and reinforce that the children made a good choice.

They have chosen to listen to the teacher. That's a good choice.

Perform a thumbs-up sign.

Relate some short scenarios and ask the pupils to put their thumbs up or down to show whether they think the action is a good choice or a poor choice.

- *You choose to hit someone. Is that a good choice or a poor choice? Thumbs up or thumbs down?*

- *You choose to share your toys with your friend. Is that a good choice or a poor choice? Thumbs up or thumbs down?*

- *You choose to tell a lie. Good choice or poor choice? Thumbs up or thumbs down?*

- *You push in the line. Good choice or poor choice? Thumbs up or thumbs down?*

- *You help to tidy up before break. Good choice or poor choice? Thumbs up or thumbs down?*

- *You call someone hurtful names. Good choice or poor choice? Thumbs up or thumbs down?*

- *You look after your friend when they are sad. Good choice or poor choice? Thumbs up or thumbs down?*

You might want to mention scenarios that have arisen recently or are pertinent to specific children in the group or to the class/school in general.

66 **When you're not sure if you're making the right choice, it's like circles in your tummy – happy and sad.** 99

Choice picture cards 10 mins.

The Choice picture cards depict scenes showing fighting, pushing in, hitting, lying, and so on.

They are designed to help pupils to practise making choices, taking part in a discussion and sharing their opinions.

Show one of the cards, e.g. telling lies, to the group.

Discuss what is happening in the picture.

Are the pupils making the right choice by hiding the ball and lying to the girl? What should they choose to do instead?

Reinforce using thumbs up and thumbs down to describe good choices and poor choices.

Give out the remaining three cards, one between two pupils. Ask them to discuss what is happening in the picture, whether the children are making a good choice or not, and, if a poor choice is depicted, what they might do instead. Allow a minute for this.

Bring the group back together and discuss the incidents on the cards, encouraging pupils to use thumbs up and thumbs down to reinforce the types of choices being made.

How do you know if you've made a right choice? We know when we have made a right choice by the feeling we have inside. So, if I told you to tell a lie, how might that make you feel? (Uncomfortable, mean, not good).

Help the pupils to recognise that how we feel inside may help us to know whether we are making a good choice or a poor choice.

If you let someone in front of you in the line and they say, 'Thank you very much', how might that make you feel?

If we listen to ourselves inside, we might feel what is right and what is wrong. Then we choose what we are going to do. We can choose to make a poor choice [thumbs down], *or we can choose to make a good choice* [thumbs up]. *Sometimes it's hard to choose.*

Can you think of a time when it was hard for you to make the right choice?

Turn to someone next to you and tell them about it.

Allow a minute for pupils to share their stories in pairs.

Well done, everyone. Sometimes it's hard to decide what the right thing to do is. We should think about how we feel inside, which will help us know what to do and make the right choice.

❝It was hard to make the right choice sometimes.❞

❝If you're doing something wrong, it feels weird inside.❞

❝I feel worried if I know someone is doing the wrong thing.❞

Colour in today's token and listen to CD [7 mins.]

To remind us to make the right choice we are each going to colour in our Right choice token.

Show the pupils the Right choice token. Each pupil colours in their token while listening to the backing track on the audio CD. Ask each pupil to write their name on the back of their token. Explain that you will keep the tokens as before, and pupils will use them soon.

Summary [5 mins.]

Who can remind us what we learned about this time? That's right, we practised making the right choices [thumbs up].

This time we are going to practise making the right choices at home and at school.

We've also got our song so we can remember what to do.

Last time, we learned how to listen well. This time we've learned how to make the right choices. Now we have two things we can do to make our school a better place.

66 There's a circle inside me and it says happy on one side and sad on the other. **99**

'We know how to ...' [10 mins.]

Teach the pupils the words and actions of the second verse of the song. Repeat together until the children can confidently join in. Sing both verses of the song with actions:

We know how to listen well ...
We know how to make the right choice ...

Next time, I'm going to ask you how you got on with making the right choice [thumbs up], *so don't forget to practise so you can tell us how you got on.*

Homework [2 mins.]

Give out homework slips.

Nominate one pupil per class to take the We make the right choices slip to their classroom.

Shall we choose whether to go out for break / lunch / back to class? Thumbs up or thumbs down?

Evaluate the session using the Adult evaluation grid for each pupil.

Right choice

Right choice

Right choice

Right choice

Right choice

Right choice

We have been working on
making the right choice.

Please praise and encourage your child when you see them making a good choice.

Your child may choose to draw a picture of themselves to show one of the times they made the right choice since Session 2.

We have been working on
making the right choice.

Please praise and encourage your child when you see them making a good choice.

Your child may choose to draw a picture of themselves to show one of the times they made the right choice since Session 2.

We have been working on
making the right choice.

Please praise and encourage your child when you see them making a good choice.

Your child may choose to draw a picture of themselves to show one of the times they made the right choice since Session 2.

Session 3: You and others

Resources

- pencils
- crayons
- Scenario cards (**PCM 16**)
- I think about others tokens (**PCM 17**)
- 'We know how to ...' lyrics, CD2 and a CD player
- Homework for Session 3 (**PCM 18**)
- We think about others classroom poster slip(s) (**PCM 11**)
- Adult evaluation grids

Aims

- To recap on last session's theme
- To know when to say sorry
- To recognise how their behaviour affects others
- To practise thinking of different ways of behaving
- To take part in a discussion and share their opinions

Introduction 1 [1 min.]

Take the register and say hello to everyone in the group.

Review homework [5 mins.]

Who is going to tell us about a good choice they made?

Who noticed that you made such a good choice?

What did they say?

Encourage pupils to share their stories and show any pictures they have drawn. Use descriptive praise to reinforce the appropriate behaviours, such as:

You made a good choice to help Rahmid with his maths. How did you decide what to do? Did you listen to your feelings and think about what your tummy felt like?

I'm sure your mum/classmate/carer noticed that you are making the right choices. I think the school must be a much better place now that you are making the right choices. I hope the other children will follow your lead. You will have to explain how to make the right choices to them.

"I think I'm doing better. I listened on the carpet and I'm enjoying my work more."

"I waited for someone in my family to finish their conversation before I asked my question."

The story continued [5 mins.]

You may wish to show the tokens from the previous sessions as a visual prompt.

Let's see what happens next in our story.

Encourage the children to join in with the following familiar sentence.

Once there was a group of children who wanted to make their school a better place.

In the first session they practised good listening [cup your hands round your ears].

In the second session they practised making the right choices [thumbs up]**.**

In the third session they decided to practise ways to make things better when they'd gone wrong.

Sometimes things go wrong no matter how hard we try. This may not be anyone's fault. Sometimes things just go wrong – I might drop my lunch on the floor accidentally, bump into someone by mistake, take a pencil without realising that someone else was using it.

What could I do to make such things better?

Encourage responses such as 'Say sorry.' In addition to saying sorry, pupils may offer solutions to the situations you gave, e.g. help to tidy up, give the pencil back, and so on. You may choose to use role-play to practise such solutions.

Game: I need some space [5 mins.]

The aim of this game is to encourage the children to be aware of others, and to take care when they are working with them.

Divide the pupils into two groups. Send one group to one end of the room and the second group to the other end. Tell all the children to shut their eyes and walk to the other side of the room carefully.

Encourage pupils to explain what they did to ensure that everyone was safe – walk slowly, hold your hands out in front of you, listen carefully, and so on.

If you don't have enough space for this version of the game, play it with the children sitting in a circle. Call out the names of two children, who then stand up, close their eyes and swap places. You can name four children in two pairs to increase the difficulty.

When we work together, we have to be careful with each other. We should try not to hurt anyone else, be kind and think about how others may be feeling. I saw how carefully you swapped places without hurting anybody in the game. We need to be just as careful with each other. Why do you think we need to be careful? Turn to the person next to you and tell them why you think we need to be careful with others.

Allow a minute for the children to share their thoughts in pairs.

Let's look at what we can do when things go wrong. First of all, we can say 'Sorry'. Next, we can see if we can make things better.

66 I'm helping more people at home and at school. 99

What should you do?
scenario cards 15 mins.

These cards depict accidents and actions with intent, and are designed to help the children think about this session's aims.

Show the scenario card about the ruined painting to the group. Choose one child from the group to help you.

We're going to pretend that I've accidentally ruined [name of child]**'s painting.**

'Oh, ..., I've ruined your work. How does that make you feel?'

Elicit response from the child, such as 'I feel cross/mad/angry.'

I'm really, really sorry.

What else might I do to make it better?

Encourage answers from the group.

I could tell the teacher it was my fault, or tidy the mess up, or help you do another painting. What would you like me to do to help make it better?

Elicit response from child.

OK, I'll help you to do a new painting. Let's get some fresh paper and get started.

Thank the child for their assistance and ask them to sit down.

So you can see, I didn't just say sorry for what happened. What else did I do? Yes, that's right, I thought of some ways that I could try to make the situation better. I let .... choose what would make them feel better and we sorted things out together. Now it's your turn.

Give out the remaining three cards, one between two pupils. Tell them they have a minute to make up a short role-play in their pairs depicting their scenario and how they might make their situation better.

Bring the group back together and ask each pair to perform their role-play. Praise the pupils who say 'Sorry', and comment on the different ideas the pairs use to try to improve their scenarios.

Praise the pairs that role-play asking their partner what type of help they would prefer, e.g:

I liked it when you let .... choose what to do. That was a very grown-up thing to do.

When things go wrong, saying sorry is very important. Sometimes, we also need to do something as well to show that we really mean it when we say 'Sorry'.

❝I understand better how what I do upsets other people sometimes.❞

Colour in today's token and listen to CD [5 mins.]

To remind us how to think about others, we are going to colour in our I think about others token.

Show the pupils the I think about others token. Each pupil colours in their token while listening to the CD. Ask each to write their name on the back of their token. Explain that you will keep them for now.

Summary [5 mins.]

Who can remind us what we learned about this time? That's right, we practised thinking [hand to head] *about others* [arm outstretched with palm up].

This time we are going to practise thinking about others at home and at school. We've also got our song so we can remember what to do.

In the first session, we learned how to listen well [cup hands round ears].

In the second session, we learned how to make the right choices [thumbs up].

This time we've learned how to think [hand to head] *about others* [arm outstretched with palm up] *at home and at school.*

Now we have three things we can do to make our school a better place.

> **"It was hard to think of answers to some of the questions."**

'We know how to ...' [10 mins.]

Teach the words and actions of the song's third verse. Repeat until the children can join in. Sing the first three verses of the song with actions:

We know how to listen well ...
We know how to make the right choice ...
We know how to think about others ...

Next time, I'm going to ask you how you got on with thinking [hand to head] *about others* [arm outstretched with palm up], *so don't forget to practise so you can tell us.*

Homework [2 mins.]

Give out homework slips. Nominate one pupil per class to take the We think about others slip to their classroom.

Let's think about all the kind things we are going to do for the other children we know on the way back to our classrooms.

Evaluate the session using the Adult evaluation grid for each pupil.

PCM 16: Scenario cards

I think about others

I think about others

I think about others

I think about others

I think about others

I think about others

Permission to Photocopy

This time we have been working on **thinking about others**.

Please praise and encourage your child when you see that they are thinking about others.

Your child may choose to draw a picture of themselves to show one of the times when they thought about others since Session 3.

This time we have been working on **thinking about others**.

Please praise and encourage your child when you see that they are thinking about others.

Your child may choose to draw a picture of themselves to show one of the times when they thought about others since Session 3.

This time we have been working on **thinking about others**.

Please praise and encourage your child when you see that they are thinking about others.

Your child may choose to draw a picture of themselves to show one of the times when they thought about others since Session 3.

Session 4: My feelings

Resources

- pencils • crayons • happy/sad signs (**PCM 19** and **20**)
- Guess the feeling poster (**PCM 21**) • Feelings cards (**PCM 22**)
- I know how I feel tokens (**PCM 23**)
- 'We know how to ...' lyrics, CD2 and a CD player
- Homework for Session 4 (**PCM 24**)
- We know how we feel classroom poster slip(s) (**PCM 11**)
- Adult evaluation grids

Aims

- To recap on last session's theme
- To recognise, name and deal with their feelings in a positive way
- To begin to think of things they can do to change how they feel
- To recognise how others may be feeling
- To take part in a discussion and share their opinions

Introduction [1 min.]

Take the register and say hello to everyone in the group.

Review homework [5 mins.]

Who would like to tell us about how they thought about others? What did you do to make someone else feel better?

Encourage and praise pupils (see Session 3):

You tried hard to make ...... feel better. You had lots of different ideas. I liked the way you asked what they would find helpful.

Who else noticed that you were thinking about others? What did they say? How did that make you feel? I'm sure your mum/ classmate/carer has noticed that you are thinking about others. The school is a better place with you thinking about other people. I hope the others will follow your lead. You will have to explain to them how to think about others as you do.

The story continued [3 mins.]

You may wish to show tokens from previous sessions as a visual prompt.

Now, back to our story. [Encourage the children to join in with ▶▶▶

▶▶▶ the following familiar sentence]. *Once there was a group of children who wanted to make their school a better place.*

In the first session they practised good listening [cup your hands round your ears].

In the second session they practised making the right choices [thumbs up].

In the third session they practised thinking [hand on head] *about others* [arm outstretched with palm up].

In the fourth session they decided to practise talking about their feelings.

Let's talk about how the people feel in the following story:

Jim fell over. He started to cry. Do you think he was happy or sad? (Sad)

Azad had pushed Jim over on purpose. Was it an accident? (No)

So how might Jim feel about that? (Angry, hurt, sad, cross)

Let's explore how we feel when things happen to us.

Game: Corners 7 mins.

This activity helps pupils to name their feelings.

Put the Happy sign and Sad sign on opposite sides of the room. Ask pupils to stand in the middle. Call out a situation and ask them to move to the sign that best represents how they feel about it. A mixed response will enable you to discuss that people may feel differently about the same situation.

Someone broke my toy.	My goldfish died.
Grandma is coming to stay.	It was my birthday.
I'm not allowed to play outside.	I got a reward certificate.
My friends chose me to be in their team.	I've lost my plimsolls.
	We had free play.

Ask the children to contribute scenarios.

Gather the group together and introduce the Guess the feeling poster.

> **66** Sometimes, if we tell the other person how we're feeling, it helps them to understand and makes it easier to sort things out. **99**

Guess the feeling 10 mins.

This activity helps pupils to identify their feelings and recognise how others might be feeling.

Invite the children to identify the feelings depicted on the poster.

Ask them to comment on when they might feel the relevant emotion, and what might cause them to feel that way.

Ask the children to show you a surprised face.

I can see from your expression that you are feeling surprised. What might make you feel like that?

Discuss their comments. Point out that people may feel differently about the same thing and that this is normal. For example, one child might feel excited about going on a school trip, whereas another child might be worried about it.

I'm going to pull a face and I want you to work out how I'm feeling.

▶▶▶

▶▶▶ Pull some faces and discuss what reasons the children have for suggesting their chosen feeling.

Call out an emotion and tell the pupils to pull a face that they think shows that emotion. Put the pupils in pairs and tell them to take turns to pull a face showing an emotion that their partner has to guess.

Ask a child to demonstrate what they think an angry person looks like.

We can tell from ......'s face that they are feeling angry. How else do we know they're angry? Yes, we can tell by what they're doing with their body too. (Clenched hands, shallow breathing, tight muscles.)

Everyone stand up and show me with your whole body what you look like when you are angry/excited/hurt/scared.

Comment on the body language demonstrated by the children.

Yes, I do that too. I put my hands to my mouth when I'm scared.

Feelings cards 10 mins.

This activity helps children think of things they can do to change outcomes. Show pupils the card of the boy receiving a present.

When I get a present it makes me feel excited and I say 'Thank you'. I'm going to show you another card and I'd like you to say how it makes you feel. [Show the illustration of the child in bed.]

Sometimes, when I'm in bed, I feel a bit scared. What could I do? What do you do when you feel like this? [Collect ideas. They may suggest: think about something nice, call my mum, switch on the light.]

Now you have a go. [Give out the cards, one between two. Give them a minute to discuss how the card makes them feel, and what they may do. Bring the group back together. Ask one child in each pair to describe their picture and the feelings they discussed. The second says what they decided they might do to help.]

Discuss each picture as a group, picking up on the idea that people can have different responses to the same situation.

One person might be excited to see a dog in the park, while another person may feel scared. It's OK to feel differently from someone else about the same situation. What is important is that you can say how you feel.

Colour in today's token and listen to CD 5 mins.

Now we're very good at describing how we feel, and knowing what we can do if we feel sad, scared or angry. We are going to colour in our feelings token to remind us to say how we feel. ▶▶▶

▸▸▸ Show the pupils the I know how I feel token. Each pupil colours in their token while listening to the CD. Ask each to write their name on the back of their token. Explain that you will keep them for now.

Summary 2 mins.

Who can remind us what we learned about this time? That's right, we practised saying how we feel [clutch hands to heart] *in different situations.*

This time we are going to practise saying how we feel at home and at school. We've also got our song so we can remember what to do.

In the first session, we learned how to listen well [cup hands round ears].

In the second session, we learned how to make the right choices [thumbs up].

In the third session, we learned how to think [hand to head] *about others* [arm outstretched with palm up] *at home and at school.*

This time we've learned how to say what we feel [clutch hands to heart].

Now we have four things we can do to make our school a better place.

66 If you feel sad inside and you don't tell anybody, you might still feel like that the next day. **99**

'We know how to ...' 10 mins.

Teach the pupils the words and actions of the fourth verse of the song. Repeat together until the children can confidently join in. Sing the first four verses of the song with actions:

We know how to listen well ...
We know how to make the right choice ...
We know how to think about others ...
We know how to say what we feel ...

Next time, I'm going to ask you to tell the group about some of the feelings you've had, and the things you did if you felt bad, so don't forget to practise so you can tell us how you got on.

Homework 2 mins.

Give out homework slips. Nominate one pupil per class to take the We know how we feel slip to their classroom.

I feel like a break, let's line up at the door and we'll go back to our classroom(s).

Evaluate the session using the Adult evaluation grid for each pupil.

PCM 21: Guess the feeling poster

PCM 22: Feelings cards

PCM 22: Feelings cards cont.

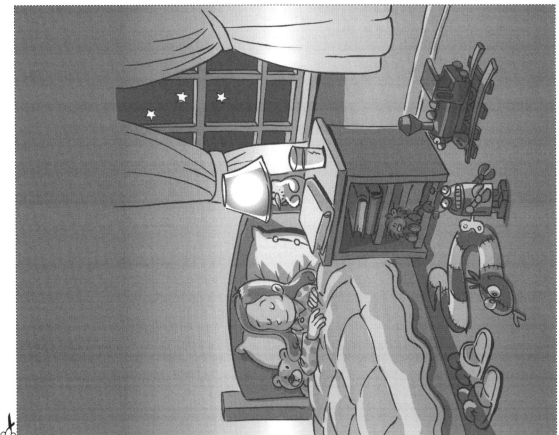

PCM 23: *I know how I feel* tokens

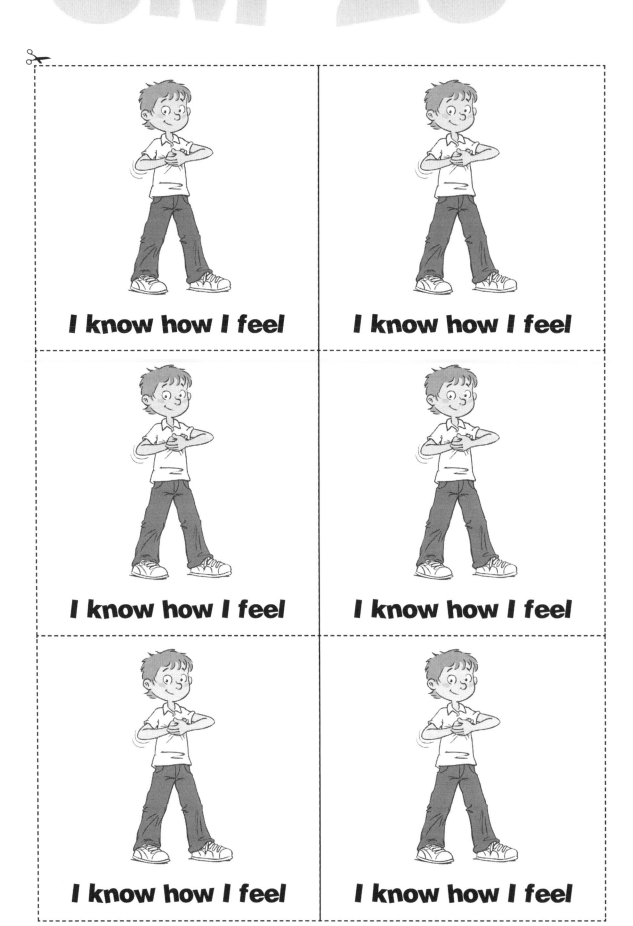

I know how I feel

I know how I feel

I know how I feel

I know how I feel

I know how I feel

I know how I feel

This time we have been working

on **feelings**.

Please praise and encourage your child when they express their feelings appropriately.

Your child may choose to draw a picture of a time when they have explained how they are feeling.

This time we have been working

on **feelings**.

Please praise and encourage your child when they express their feelings appropriately.

Your child may choose to draw a picture of a time when they have explained how they are feeling.

This time we have been working

on **feelings**.

Please praise and encourage your child when they express their feelings appropriately.

Your child may choose to draw a picture of a time when they have explained how they are feeling.

Session 5: We are special

Resources

- pencils
- crayons
- Guess the feeling poster (**PCM 21**)
- I am special tokens (**PCM 25**)
- Homework for Session 5 (**PCM 26**)
- 'We know how to ...' lyrics, CD2 and a CD player
- We are special classroom poster slip(s) (**PCM 11**)
- Adult evaluation grids

Aims

- To recap on last session's theme
- To identify and respect the similarities and differences between people
- To take part in a discussion and share their opinions

Introduction 1 min.

Take the register and say hello to everyone in the group.

Review homework 5 mins.

Last time we learned how to say how we feel. Which feelings did we practise?

Refer to the Guess the feeling poster to remind the group.

You went away to think about all the different feelings you have and what you can do if you feel bad, sad, angry or scared. Choose one feeling you had and tell us about what happened.

Focus on appropriate responses and encourage description of feelings with questions such as:

So what did you do to stop yourself from feeling scared?

Fantastic, I like the way you can tell me how you feel, and all the ideas you've had to make things better if you're feeling bad.

The story continued 5 mins.

You may wish to show tokens from previous sessions as a visual prompt.

Now it's time to carry on with our story:

Encourage the children to join in with the following familiar sentence. ▶▶▶

▶▶▶ *Once there was a group of children who wanted to make their school a better place.*

In the first session they practised good listening [cup your hands round your ears].

In the second session they practised making the right choice [thumbs up].

In the third session they practised thinking [hand on head] *about others* [arm outstretched with palm up].

In the fourth session they practised talking about their feelings [clutch hands to heart].

Next, they decided to think about how sometimes we are the same and sometimes we are different, and that's OK.

Game: Guess who 10 mins.

This game shows that we have some characteristics that are the same, although we are also different.

Ask pupils to stand in a circle. Describe someone in the group and ask the children to work out who it is.

Who am I talking about? This person is wearing school uniform. They have two eyes, black shoes, brown hair and are wearing glasses.

Adapt this to suit your group, keeping the initial clues generic. Allow the children to guess.

How did you know? Everyone is wearing school uniform and black shoes.

Discuss how there are some things about us all that are usually the same and some things that are different – that's what makes us special.

Now it's your go.

Choose a child to describe and allow pupils to guess. Repeat with another child. Ask the group to sit down.

This time, instead of describing what we look like, we're going to describe what kind of people we are. Sit with your eyes closed and think about what sort of person you are. You might describe yourself as kind, helpful, a good friend, clever, sporty, sometimes angry, funny. If I asked one of your friends to describe you, what do you think they might say? Open your eyes when you have thought of how someone else might describe you.

Allow each pupil to say a word or phrase to describe themselves.

Well done. Now let's see how other people in the group would describe you. What sort of person is ......?

Set the tone by modelling the first comment for each child. Confirm the pupil's positive qualities, e.g. *'She is friendly because she lets me join in her games.'*

I think ...... is helpful because she stays in at playtime to help me tidy up sometimes. What do you want to say?

Rephrase any negative comments to normalise them: *Yes, lots of people get fed up when they have to keep stopping their game.*

If a pupil doesn't wish to be described, say a few brief sentences about their positive qualities and move on.

❝My mum said she was proud of me and I felt really happy.❞

Game: If 5 mins.

This game reinforces similarities and differences.

Ask the group to sit in a circle and respond to your instructions. Some examples follow:

- If you've got brown eyes, swap places.
- If you're kind, stamp your feet.
- If you're wearing a skirt, stand up, turn round and sit down.
- If you have a brother, wave your arms in the air.

Choose any descriptions that are pertinent to specific children you are working with. Invite the pupils to suggest some statements.

I am special 5 mins.

We've looked at lots of ways that we are like each other. Now each of us in turn is going to say one thing that's different about us, one thing that makes us special. You can choose what you think it is that makes you special. It might be the way you look or something special that you do. [If appropriate, include differences relating to culture, disability, religion, and so on.]

Describe yourself first as a model statement.

I'm special because I love teaching children / have red hair / love my dog and take it for a walk every day / take my mum shopping.

Encourage members of the group to share their statement, supporting those who may have difficulty.

This time we talked about how we are the same and how we are different – our similarities and our differences – and what makes us special. We are special to lots of people, such as friends and family. Who else thinks you're special?

Allow group members to share examples.

You can see that we are special to lots of people and that's a very nice feeling.

> 66 Now, my friends play with me more because they want to be in the group. 99

> 66 He's a good partner to have in class because he's fun to work with. 99

Colour in today's token and listen to CD 5 mins.

We are going to colour in our I am special token to remind us how special we are.

Show the pupils the I am special token. Each pupil colours in their token while listening to the CD. Ask each to write their name on the back of their token. Explain that you will keep them for now.

> 66 She's friendly and cheerful. 99

Summary [5 mins.]

Who can remind us what we learned about this time? We thought about how we are similar and how we are different and all the ways that we are special. This is how we show we are special [hands clenched and shake above the head].

We've got our song so we can remember what we've learned this week.

In the first session, we learned how to listen well [cup hands round ears].

In the second session, we learned how to make the right choices [thumbs up].

In the third session, we learned how to think [hand to head] *about others* [arm outstretched with palm up] *at home and at school.*

In the fourth session, we learned how to say what we feel [clutch hands to heart].

This time we've learned how special we are [clasp hands above head].

Now we have five things we can do to make our school a better place.

> **She's very kind and she helps people if they can't do their maths.**

'We know how to ...' [10 mins.]

Teach the pupils the words and actions of the fifth verse of the song. Repeat together until the children can confidently join in. Sing the first five verses of the song with actions:

We know how to listen well ...
We know how to make the right choice ...
We know how to think about others ...
We know how to say what we feel ...
We know that we are special ...

Next time, I'm going to ask you to tell the group about something you did the same or differently from your friends and what happened, so don't forget to practise so you can tell us how you got on.

Homework [2 mins.]

Give out homework slips. Nominate one pupil per class to take the We are special slip to their classroom.

Let's line up at the door and we'll go back by a different route from the one we normally take. We'll do something different because we're special.

Evaluate the session using the Adult evaluation grid for each pupil.

I am special

I am special

I am special

I am special

I am special

I am special

This time we have been working on

we are special.

Please make your child feel special.
Your child may choose to draw a picture of a time when they felt special.

This time we have been working on

we are special.

Please make your child feel special.
Your child may choose to draw a picture of a time when they felt special.

This time we have been working on

we are special.

Please make your child feel special.
Your child may choose to draw a picture of a time when they felt special.

Session 6:
Working and playing together

Resources

- pencils
- crayons
- Discussion cards (**PCM 27**)
- We know how to work and play together tokens (**PCM 28**)
- 'We know how to ...' lyrics, CD2 and a CD player
- Homework for Session 6 (**PCM 29**)
- We work and play together classroom poster slip(s) (**PCM 11**)
- Adult evaluation grids

Aims

- To recap on last session's theme
- To play and work cooperatively
- To recognise what is fair and unfair
- To take part in a discussion and share their opinions

Introduction 1 min.

Take the register and say hello to everyone in the group.

Review homework 5 mins.

Last time we talked about our similarities and differences – the ways in which we are the same, the ways in which we are different, and the things that make us special.

I want you to tell us something that you realised was the same about you and someone else, and something that was different.

Give a model sentence, such as:

I played football in the garden with my children. We played the same game together. Then they had some chocolate, but I didn't because I don't like chocolate, so I was different.

Who wants to tell us about something that they realised was the same or different last time?

As you ask each group member to speak, encourage them to reflect on what they did, how it felt and how it's all right to be different, for example:

How was it when you decided to be different?

How did your brother feel when you didn't want to play?

▶▶▶

▶▶▶ *Sometimes it feels good to do the same as everyone else. It can be hard to be different and you don't have to be, but if it feels right, then that's OK. Everyone is the same in lots of ways and different in lots of ways. That's what makes us special.*

The story continued 3 mins.

You may wish to show tokens from previous sessions as a visual prompt.

Now it's time to carry on with our story.

Encourage the children to join in with the following familiar sentence.

Once there was a group of children who wanted to make their school a better place.

In the first session they practised good listening [cup your hands round your ears].

In the second session they practised making the right choice [thumbs up].

In the third session they practised thinking [hand on head] *about others* [arm outstretched with palm up].

In the fourth session they practised talking about their feelings [clutch hands to heart].

In the fifth session they decided to think about how sometimes we are the same and sometimes we are different, and that's OK [clasp hands above head].

The last thing they practised was playing together and working together.

Tangles 10 mins.

This game encourages cooperation, listening skills and teamwork.

Ask everyone to stand in an inward-facing circle and hold the hand of the person on either side of them. Say **'3, 2, 1, let's get tangled!'** Pupils move towards the centre of the circle, weaving in between each other's arms, taking care not to let go of their partners' hands or hurt each other. After a few seconds, call **'Freeze'**.

Give the group verbal instructions to help them untangle themselves without breaking any of the linked hands.

Once they are untangled, ask **'How did we work out the solution?'** Answers could include by cooperating, listening to each other, trying different ways, working together.

Play the game again, allowing a pupil to untangle the group.

Ask the group to sit down and recap on the skills that were used to play the game successfully.

What did you have to do to be successful at that game?

Suggestions might include: listen to the leader, listen to each other, don't let go of your partners, look after each other, be patient, follow instructions, wait for your turn.

Many of these are the skills we need to work and play together well. Let's practise these skills now.

Discussion cards 10 mins.

These cards depict different dilemmas for discussion purposes. This activity helps pupils to recognise what is fair and unfair. Choose a discussion card to discuss together. Prompt the discussion by asking questions such as:

- *What do you think should happen?*
- *How do they feel?*
- *What might they do to sort it out?*
- *How might they say that without upsetting their friend?*

The pupils may respond with answers such as, 'Say "No"', 'Say "Next time"', 'Say "Yes, OK"', 'Ask them to play with ....'.

Do you think what we decided was fair? I think it was fair because we thought about it and decided together, and most people thought it was the best thing to do.

Put the children in pairs and give each pair a discussion card. Allow a minute for the pairs to discuss what is happening in their picture and what they think is a fair solution to the problem.

Bring the group back together. Ask the pairs to describe what is happening in their picture and what they think is a fair solution to the problem.

Support the discussion by using questions such as:

- *I like that idea. Do you have any other ideas?*
- *What made you choose that way to work things out?*
- *Does anyone in the group have a different idea?*
- *Why do you think that idea was fair?*

Well done, you've thought carefully about what is fair and what isn't fair, and what we can do about it. Sometimes we feel that things aren't fair, but there's nothing we can do about it. For example, I dropped my ice cream on the floor, so I had no ice cream and there was no more left. I was sad and it didn't feel fair, but there was nothing I could do, so I went and got a drink instead.

> 66 We sorted things out by talking and I explained how I felt. 99

Colour in today's token and listen to CD 5 mins.

We are going to colour in our We know how to work and play together token to remind us how we get along with other people.

Show the pupils the We know how to work and play together token. Each pupil colours in their token while listening to the backing track on the audio CD. Ask each pupil to write their name on the back of their token. Explain that you will keep the tokens, and pupils will use them soon.

Summary [5 mins.]

Who can remind us what we learned about this time? Yes, we learned how to work and play together. This is how we show we can work and play together [swing arms backwards and forwards by your sides].

We've also got our song so we can remember what we've learned.

In the first session, we learned how to listen well [cup hands round ears].

In the second session, we learned how to make the right choices [thumbs up].

In the third session, we learned how to think [hand to head] *about others* [arm outstretched with palm up] *at home and at school.*

In the fourth session, we learned how to say what we feel [clutch hands to heart].

In the fifth session, we learned how special we are [clasp hands above head].

This time we learned how to work and play together [swing arms backwards and forwards].

Now we have six things we can do to make our school a better place.

"I made a new friend this week."

'We know how to ...' [10 mins.]

Teach the pupils the words and actions of the sixth verse of the song. Repeat together until the children can confidently join in. Sing the six verses of the song with actions:

We know how to listen well ...
We know how to make the right choice ...
We know how to think about others ...
We know how to say what we feel ...
We know that we are special ...
We know how to work and play together ...

Next time, I'm going to ask you to tell the group about how you got on working and playing together, so don't forget to practise so you can tell us.

Homework [2 mins.]

Give out homework slips.

Nominate one pupil per class to take the We work and play together slip to their classroom.

Next session is our last together and we're going to make our special poster so that we can help to make our school a better place.

Let's line up at the door to leave.

Evaluate the session using the Adult evaluation grid for each pupil.

PCM 27: Discussion cards

**We know how
to work and play
together**

**We know how
to work and play
together**

**We know how
to work and play
together**

**We know how
to work and play
together**

**We know how
to work and play
together**

**We know how
to work and play
together**

Permission to Photocopy

This time we have been working on

working and playing together.

Please praise and encourage your child when you see them playing or working well with others.

Your child may choose to draw a picture of a time when they worked or played well with someone.

This time we have been working on

working and playing together.

Please praise and encourage your child when you see them playing or working well with others.

Your child may choose to draw a picture of a time when they worked or played well with someone.

This time we have been working on

working and playing together.

Please praise and encourage your child when you see them playing or working well with others.

Your child may choose to draw a picture of a time when they worked or played well with someone.

Session 7:
Making our school a better place

Resources

- pencils • crayons • glue
- glitter and other forms of decoration
- each child's set of coloured-in tokens
- Pupil poster (**PCM 30**) – one per pupil
- Certificate of achievement (**PCM 31**) – one each
- Pupil self-rating questionnaires (filled in before Session 1)
- small stickers for pupils to use on their questionnaires
- 'We know how to ...' lyrics, CD2 and a CD player
- Adult evaluation grids

Aims

- To recap on last session's theme
- To recap on the themes from the previous sessions
- To make the children's posters and reflect on progress
- To discuss how pupils can continue to make their school a better place
- To complete the Pupil self-rating questionnaires
- To thank the group for their participation, and present them with their posters, certificates of achievement and gifts (if appropriate)

Introduction 1 min.

Take the register and greet everyone.

Review homework 5 mins.

Last time you practised working and playing together well. Who would like to tell us how they got on?

Encourage the children to reflect on what they did, how it felt, what they might do differently next time, who noticed that they worked well together.

The story continued 5 mins.

You may wish to show the tokens from the previous sessions as a visual prompt.

Today we're going to finish our story and see what the children did next.

Encourage the children to join in with the following familiar sentence.

Once there was a group of children who wanted to make their school a better place.

In the first session they practised good listening [cup your hands round your ears]**.**

In the second session they practised making the right choice [thumbs up]**.**

In the third session they practised thinking [hand on head] **about others** [arm outstretched with palm up]**.**

In the fourth session they practised talking about their feelings [clutch hands to heart]**.**

In the fifth session they decided to think about how sometimes we are the same and sometimes we are different, and that's OK [clasp hands above head]**.**

The last thing they practised was playing together and working together [swing arms backwards and forwards]**.**

And do you know what? Yes, they did make their school a better place, and they showed all the other children how to do the good things they had learned. Then they each made a poster to remind themselves and all the other children what they had learned. We're going to make our posters today. You're going to take all of the tokens that you coloured in so beautifully and stick them on to your own poster.

Making the pupil posters 10 mins.

Pupils stick their tokens on to their poster, write their name in the space provided and decorate as appropriate.

You may like to refer to the glitter as 'magic glitter' that helps pupils to remember how to make their school a better place.

Pupil evaluation 10 mins.

This activity encourages self-evaluation and reflection.

Give each pupil the copy of the Pupil self-rating questionnaire that they filled in before the programme started, and eight stickers.

▶▶▶

▶▶▶ ***Who remembers this form? Yes, you each filled one in before we started meeting together. You can see where you put your stickers then to show how you felt about some things. Let's look at the first statement, 'I am able to express my feelings'.***

Point to the sticker that you put on the line alongside this statement.

That's how you felt before we started these sessions. We want to find out how you feel now. Think about where you want to put your new sticker on the same line.

Will it be in the same place as before, or do you think you're better at expressing your feelings now?

Point to where you think your sticker should go now.

You don't need to look at what anyone else is doing, just think about your own feelings. Well done. Now, stick your sticker where you've decided it should go.

Encourage the children to be honest in their responses.

Continue in the same way until each pupil has completed their questionnaire. Do not acknowledge or discuss any of the children's judgements.

Well done, everyone. Now we're going to talk about how we've got on in our group.

Note down each pupil's responses in the appropriate section of their Adult evaluation grid.

Go round the group and ask each pupil to share their thoughts on the following:

- something I learned
- something I found difficult
- something I do differently now
- something I enjoyed.

The following quotes are some of the responses children have given:

Something I learned

- How to tell people not to say things about me.
- How special people can be.
- Instead of thinking everything is easy for others, it may not be that easy for them.
- It's important to be nice to others.
- Not to fight as much.
- To think about others.
- I enjoyed everything!

Something I do differently now

- I tell the teacher if someone does something wrong to me – before, I would have hit them.
- I can think more about others.
- Instead of just telling a teacher, I try to sort it out myself.
- I try to cheer someone up if they are upset.
- If someone breaks something, I tell them to be careful because it hurts people's feelings.

▶▶▶

▶▶▶ **Something I found difficult**

- It's hard always making the right choice.
- I got mixed up in my feelings.

Something I enjoyed

- Everything!
- The games
- Making the poster
- Singing the song
- Playing Tangles
- The happy and sad game
- Everything, especially the games – they taught me how to work with others
- When other people noticed me coming back from the group and wanted to know what we'd been doing
- The group – it helped me with my own problems because I heard what other people would do

Pupil reflection 5 mins.

This is an opportunity for pupils to reflect on what they have learned.

Thank you for sharing your thoughts. Let's look at your lovely posters and remind ourselves what we have learned.

We're going to go round the group and I'd like each of you to show us your favourite bit of your poster and talk about one thing you will do to help make our school a better place.

Ask for specific examples, such as *'Playing well with your friends is a great idea. How will you make sure that happens?'*

'We know how to ...' 10 mins.

We've got two things to remind us how to make our school a better place. We've got our wonderful posters, which I'm going to laminate so that they will last before you take them away.

We've also got our song. Let's remind ourselves of the words before we sing it together for the last time.

In the first session, we learned how to listen well [cup hands round ears].

In the second session, we learned how to make the right choices [thumbs up].

In the third session, we learned how to think [hand to head] *about others* [arm outstretched with palm up] *at home and at school.*

In the fourth session, we learned how to say what we feel [clutch hands to heart].

▶▶▶

▶▶▶ *In the fifth session, we learned how special we are* [clasp hands above head].

In the sixth session, we learned how to work and play together [swing arms backwards and forwards].

So, now we have a whole song to remind us all what we can do to make our school a better place.

Sing the complete song with actions together:

We know how to listen well ...
We know how to make the right choice ...
We know how to think about others ...
We know how to say what we feel ...
We know that we are special ...
We know how to work and play together ...

Celebrating achievement 5 mins.

This activity recognises the individual effort pupils have made and their contribution to the achievements of the group.

Congratulate the group on how well they have worked together and individually.

Present each child with their Certificate of achievement and any other rewards the school may decide to give.

You may decide to hold a formal ceremony to mark the end of the group's programme. Some schools hold a class or whole-school assembly during which pupils show their posters, talk about the work they have done in the group and teach the rest of the class or school the 'We know how to ...' song with actions.

Final game 5 mins.

Finish on a light-hearted note by playing the children's favourite game from one of the previous sessions. It's usually Tangles!

Final evaluation

At the end of the programme the adult running the group, together with the relevant class teacher(s) should rate the pupils again using the Adult skills-rating form, which they filled in at the start of the programme.

You can then look at your findings, along with the other records from the programme, and discuss with the relevant staff members whether any further action is appropriate (see p.11).

PCM 30: Pupil poster

Photocopy both pages on A3 card to make each pupil's poster.

We are making our school a better place.

Name

....

School

....

....

I HELPED TO
MAKE MY SCHOOL A
BETTER PLACE

Presented to

....

by

....

Date ....